Nothing Grows in One Place Forever

Books by LEO LUKE MARCELLO

Poetry

Blackrobe's Love Letters   (1994)

The Secret Proximity of Everywhere   (1994)

Silent Film   (1997)

Nothing Grows in One Place Forever: Poems of a Sicilian American   (1998)

Also by the Author

Everything Comes to Light: A Festschrift for Joy Scantlebury   (1993)

NOTHING GROWS IN ONE PLACE FOREVER

POEMS OF A SICILIAN AMERICAN

LEO LUKE MARCELLO

TIME BEING BOOKS
POETRY IN SIGHT AND SOUND
St. Louis, Missouri

Copyright © 1998 by Leo Luke Marcello

All rights reserved under International and Pan-American Copyright Conventions. No part of this book shall be reproduced in any form (except by reviewers for the public press) without written permission from the publisher:

Time Being Books®
10411 Clayton Road
St. Louis, Missouri 63131

Time Being Books® is an imprint of Time Being Press®
St. Louis, Missouri

Time Being Press® is a 501(c)(3) not-for-profit corporation.

Time Being Books® volumes are printed on acid-free paper, and binding materials are chosen for strength and durability.

ISBN 1-56809-036-6 (Hardcover)
ISBN 1-56809-037-4 (Paperback)

Library of Congress Cataloging-in-Publication Data:

Marcello, Leo Luke, 1945–
    Nothing grows in one place forever : poems of a Sicilian American / Leo Luke Marcello. — 1st ed.
        p.   cm.
    ISBN 1-56809-036-6 (hardcover : alk. paper). — ISBN 1-56809-037-4 (pbk. : alk. paper)
    1. Italian Americans—Poetry. 2. Sicily (Italy)—Emigration and immigration —Poetry. I. Title.
PS3563.A6327N68   1998
811'.54—dc21   98-11360
                                                                                   CIP

Cover art by Chris Marcello, *The Great Storm*
Book design and typesetting by Sheri L. Vandermolen
Manufactured in the United States of America

First Edition, first printing (September 1998)

Acknowledgments

I wish to acknowledge these publications, in which the following poems appeared: *America* ("Drinking from a Paper Cup"); *Anthology of Magazine Verse and Yearbook of American Poetry* ("Villanelle on the Suicide of a Young Belgian Teacher Soon to Be Naturalized" and "William Faulkner, Sacred Cow"); *Burning Light* ("The Burning Bush"); *Cedar Rock* ("A Fig Tree"); *Chester H. Jones 1991 Anthology* ("Edward Hopper's *Cape Cod Morning*, 1950"); *Commonweal* ("Times Your Aunt Mary Needs You"); *Context South* ("Fireflies and the Dry Cleaners"); *Epos* [now *Alabama Literary Review*] ("On the Birth and Death of My Sister's Son Jared," "Parade Ground," and "Snow Goose"); *First Things* ("Remembering the *Titanic* Every April 15"); *Greenfield Review* ("Use the Common Present to Report What a Person or Thing Does Regularly" and "Using the Common Future to Report What Will Happen Under Certain Conditions"); *Gulf Coast Collection of Stories and Poems* ("Among Cherry Blossoms"); *Houston Poetry Fest Anthology* ("E lucevan le stelle"); *Immortelles: Poems of Life and Death by New Southern Writers* ("Drinking from a Paper Cup"); *In the West of Ireland* ("Lost: Paperweight, Rose Rhodochrosite on Malachite"); *Journeymen* ("The Swan Room, 1957"); *Louisiana English Journal* ("A Sonata of Things You'll Never Know"); *Louisiana Literature* ("Good Wine Wasted and a Place to Rest," "Her Wallpaper," and "The Loop, Chincoteague, Virginia"); *The Maple Leaf Rag Fifteenth Anniversary Anthology* ("Boxes of Books"); *New Delta Review* ("E lucevan le stelle"); *North Stone Review* ("The Infinite Possibilities of Desire" and "Local Peaches"); *Ordinary Time* ("Resurrection Scherzo"); *Poetry NOW* ("Burning Leaves"); *The Prose Poem* ("The Man Who Picked Up Nails"); *The Southern Review* ("Buying Cheese," "The Parking Lot," "Villanelle on the Suicide of a Young Belgian Teacher Soon to Be Naturalized," and "William Faulkner, Sacred Cow"); *Studia Mystica* ("Visiting My Cousin"); *Times Picayune* ("Boxes of Books"); *Uncommonplace: An Anthology of Contemporary Louisiana Poets* ("The Behavior of Ants"); *Westview: A Journal of Western Oklahoma* ("Rocky and Mary Time"); and *Xavier Review* ("The Photographer, Wrestling with Words").

In memory of my father,
Luke M. Marcello

Who would have thought my shrivel'd heart
Could have recover'd greennesse?
— George Herbert

CONTENTS

Relatives and Friends

Students in Worlds That No Longer Exist

Love Lessons

LAST WORDS

NOTHING GROWS IN
ONE PLACE FOREVER

IMMIGRANTS

Was it for this the wild geese spread
The grey wing upon every tide . . .
— William Butler Yeats

Anna and the Great Storm

1: Immigration and Burial at Sea

Your mother had died in the Old Country.
Father and brother had crossed the ocean.
They waited for you on the other side.
Still a child yourself, you cradled
the baby brother in your arms
and led the twin sisters onto the ship.

The ocean was bigger than you knew.
Fevers raged and the baby died,
taken from your arms and buried at sea.
You screamed, hysterical
until some old woman
— you never named her for me —
slapped you.

When the ship arrived in the New World,
your father and your older brother met you.
You stood a little taller than the twins.
Your arms were empty.

2: The Great Storm

Galveston, Texas, September 8, 1900

At eighteen you saw the Great Beast
rise up again out of the water,
the Great Storm, they called it,
that destroyed Galveston.

Six thousand dead, the paper counted,
though no one knew for sure,
perhaps that many more.

The beach hotels were full.
Tourists watched the waves roll
in, the sky blackening out the Gulf,
rolling in and cutting off the island.
Escape was impossible.
Into the night the waters rose.
Houses ripped apart in the wind,
planks flying, people torn
from windows and roofs,
floors disintegrating.

All night you prayed
in the crowded church,
while the hurricane raged,
battering houses, ripping foundations.
A cow was hurled into an upstairs bedroom,
a woman crushed beneath the roof
her children were tied to,
but not discovered
until daybreak,

a morning out of Dante's hell,
a drenched city in ruins,
bodies turning up everywhere in the debris,
stacked nameless in warehouses.

The sea kept spitting back
those buried there — and others,
naked bodies, children, men, and women,
torn from the roofs the furious
night before.

In the ensuing days people burned
on the spot whomever the sea spat
out, others buried wherever found.

The island became its own burial
ground, its air death-choked,
its sand dug into for bones.
In the months after, the whole island
was raised, tons of wet sand brought
up out of the Gulf, spread level,
so deep no one planting a garden
will ever turn up bones
in years to come.

3: Honeymoon Apples

The train windowpanes rattled.
It turned into a long ride.
Liborio sat with the honeymoon
apples shaking on his lap,
a bag he reached into from town
to town.

Later, in the sawmill camps,
she would cook suppers
for a campful of
strangers.

Would he thank her then?
He had had his fill of the honeymoon
apples, while she waited, hungry.
Did other American brides shake
on this track?

She dreamed, empty.
Her children would
have their fill.

4: The Kitchen Table

My father was your fourth child.
The fifth, he remembered, they took from you
and placed on the kitchen table,
opened its throat with a knife.

Butchers, you screamed.
When they returned it to your arms,
it was no longer a little boy.
Butcher, you called the doctor.

My father remembered the short coffin
but not the little brother.
You had another in a year
and named him Antonio also,

as if there had never been
another child lost at sea
or a son who died to diphtheria.
Butcher, you screamed from the long bed
and rang a bell from the back of the house.
The kitchen table was never the same.

Years after you were dead,
a photograph of the young priest
emerged from your dining-room drawer,
two pinholes in his eyes
and a large X scratched
lightly across his smile.

I do not know what
you called him,

but the little boys
were always Tony,

for St. Anthony,
patron of lost things.

5: The Ax-Man

One night the Ax-Man slipped
into your sister Mary's house.
He split her husband's head,
and before she could escape,
the ax had slashed her face.
She moved away.
I never met her.
I never saw her scar.

Years later I stared at the tin roof,
rusting under the heat of the sun,
the silvery-white tin splotched
blood-reddish-brown, time-oxidized.
Trees and weeds grew up through the floor.
People said it was haunted, but I knew
better. It was only cursed.

Aunt Pidda, your other sister, visited
summers in her old age. She was
a tiny copy of you but animated
like an old doll given life
and a little-girl laugh
that would never grow old.
Her husband had a thick mustache,
thick as white taffy.
Ziu Caliddu, we called him.
He smoked an exotic, curled pipe
and dangled a fine watch
on a golden chain.

Grown up, I traveled to see her once.
Ziu Caliddu was dead, but Aunt Pidda's house
smelled as sweet and foreign as Ziu Caliddu's smoke.

She spoke excitedly in the Dialect.
I couldn't understand. I could.
She laughed the little-girl laugh
and smiled, her blue-gray eyes twinkling
as she touched my face
and each one of my fingers
as if making a pentagram
or star or making sure
I'd been born with all
that was coming to me.

6: Coma

I remember you standing only once.
We'd moved into our new house.
You came with Aunt Bennie.
You sat at our green formica table
and drank coffee.
Your black veil was lacy.
You smiled. We were thrilled.
It seemed a miracle
you were not in bed.

You walked into our new kitchen.
You sat at our new table,
enjoyed coffee and perhaps
a piece of cake.

The last three years of your life,
you slept the diabetic coma,
silenced by strokes,
fed by tubes.

Your skin remained pink.
Your gray eyes did not see.

"Bless us," we greeted you
in the old language, anyway,
waiting, as always, hoping
that one day you'd open
your eyes and answer again
the Dialectical blessing.

7: Spiders and Shoes

The night before the coma,
you called your dead
husband's name.

You cried for shoes.

There were spiders on your face,
you screamed.

We sat on the living-room floor.
On the other side of the closed door,
the priest prayed over you
with your grown children.

I thought the door would never open
or, if it opened, the room would be
on fire with the heat of God
and of his angels
and of his saints.

8: Procession

In the car Aunt Bennie said,
It's been years since Mama
passed this way.

She meant the street,
the buildings, the views.
The words struck odd.
What if the sidewalks moved
and we stood still?
Would the passing
be any different?

She said it blankly,
without tears.
Later she cried,
and the room Nonna had lived
and died in remained closed.
Sometimes we would slip through it.
It smelled clean, and there was
never any heat in it.
I decided after that

the light of angels was not hot
and that if I ever heard
the Dialectical response
of *Santu*, it would be
the voice of God, and
it would be
in this room.

9: Revelations

I, ninety-two years after the fact,
resurrected this one frightening bone,
not out of the old sands of new Galveston beach
but within the pages of a recent magazine,
pressed like a forgotten rose
but still grisly with the facts
of history and the Great Storm.

St. Anthony, finder of lost things,
what a discovery —

a discovery, as if among dried sinews,
as if caught, like a desiccated nerve,
lying untouched in the foramen
where it had once sent
impulses to a living mind,
the electrical message:

On the day you endured
the island's destruction,
the eighth of September, 1900,
you celebrated another turning.

It was your eighteenth birthday.

Frayed Papers

Months after the funeral, she found
stacked in cardboard boxes
the yellowed immigration papers.
The facts uncurled with the flowery script:

her father's name, his father's name, and
her father's father's and her father's mother's
and her father's widowed sister's and the orphans'
and the dates of the departure.

The sixth of January, a likely feast,
another Epiphany, unlikely.

The tickets have grown thin,
limp as a wet leaf, but dry,
tiny fragile slips of paper,
senseless, really, how such fragments
could portend so much — the dreams,
the new beginnings. Did they really
look out across that gray ocean
and believe the future more
than cardboard boxes?

Scratched Faces

Nonna's face scratched
from the family photograph
lay hidden in the bottom drawer
of the mahogany secretary

except for the occasional airing
it got when Aunt Bennie let us
rummage the faces of the dead.

There are other copies
of this photograph,
unmarked, unscratched,
as if someone had fought
hard to preserve the memory
of what can't be obliterated
by a hat pin or angry fingernail.

Kissing My Hand

My great-great-granddaughter brags.
Her little classmates hiss.
Not royalty, they cannot comprehend
but fear the regal blood that connects
this child to me, her great-great-
grandmother.

People kissed my hand and rightly so.
They rolled the "r" in my name
and kissed this soft, strong hand
because I am descended from one
of the ancient noble families
of our island.

Do not even dare think it.
Ours was not an evil rule.

I may be long dead,
but I can still
hear your thoughts.

The Will

Within the folded, yellowing envelope
is an equally yellowing cellophane,
and within the fragile cellophaned envelope,
on folded, lightly blue-lined paper,
the elegant script of my grandfather's
last wishes, the page neatly squared
as it parceled unequal real estate.

My father's brothers and sisters got more.
My father's education was his piece of land.
He told me that one Christmas the rest
of them got cash in their envelopes.
He got a hug. His degree was supposed
to be his bag of gold. He told me
that later he cried.

The others could have had an education,
if they'd wanted, and anyway, he'd worked
hard. In this new country, equality
was the dream. They all dreamed.

Within these layered envelopes,
I keep this ancient Sicilian will.

They are all dead, the land all gone.
There is a slight smudge across the paper,
a wet spot, as if the ink had smeared
with a stray drop of rain or been
smudged by a damp finger.

The Parking Lot

In the big two-storied house
with the swing on the front porch,
horseshoe over the back door,
yard full of trees and hedges,
pecan, hydrangeas, orange, fig,
chicken coop and pen to the rear,
quiet streets along the side and front,
people used to come from all over the state,
sometimes at dinner twenty-five around the table,
laughing, feasting on pasta or homemade sausage,
singing Old Country songs, drinking to the future.

At the head of the table,
the old man, cracking chestnuts,
settled family arguments while
children danced in the living room
to clarinet and accordion and while
Nonna, unable to walk, waved her hand
in the front bedroom overlooking the street.
She called us to enter her room, which was filled
with sunlight and statues, and she begged us to dance,
singing with us as we danced for her, laughing, her only way.
Once, in my excitement, I knocked a saint over, breaking it
into hundreds of white chips, and I began to cry until
she said, smiling, "Dance, child. Make the saints happy."
For the last years of her life, she was asleep,
eyes closed. The house is no longer there.

In the Old Country the Cappuccini monks
used to hang the dead in hallways of the convent,
propping them against the walls or laying them on tables.
The living visited the dead, changing the burial clothes,
discussing family troubles until the sight was unbearable,
death-smiles peeling away with the skin, bones protruding,
until it became easier to talk at home, in a street, in a garden.
But this is not the Old Country, and no one hangs in hallways.

When Aunt Bennie was dying,
her Pentecostal neighbors came to the hospital,
afraid they would not get the land next to their church.
Their fears were groundless, for no one could take her place.
When she died, they bought her house and land and sold the
    house

to a man who took it to another town. Then they dug up the trees
and laid their smooth gray surface of a parking lot
where now not even one foot of earth is exposed except
for the squares in the cement where tiny shrubs grow
in the shadow of Cadillacs and Pentecostal tongues.

The day the movers came,
I was standing across the street,
which had been turned into a busy one-way,
and I watched the house moving in three pieces
at the very center of a solemn parade,
a truck of cable-lifters, shouting,
the backed-up line of cars, overheating,
the flashing lights of a police-car,
warning cars and people, anyone
who might be going too fast.

FAMILY HISTORY

Lacrimae rerum — There are tears in things.
— Virgil

Burning Leaves

Father,
in an instant
the odor of burning leaves
brings you back to me,

standing by the metal cans
where you stirred up smoke
from the cinder-hot
pecan-leaf inferno

singeing some back-hidden
pleasure center of our brains
by sending pungent arrows
of pulsing fire-clouds
up through breath

a cold winter day years ago,
when you were alive and
burning leaves out back
was legal.

Buying Cheese

We are going to buy some cheese,
our usual last-minute souvenir
of summer vacations in New Orleans.
In the large, almost empty store,
my father speaks in the old language,
an old music full of u's and d's,
occasional slapping of tongue.

We consider the shelves,
gallon-bottles of ripe olives,
small yellow cans of *pasta con sarde*,
red and white cans of imported sardines,
a high stack of old newspapers,
a heavy steel cash register.

The owner takes us back
into the cool, dark storage
full of the smells of cheese,
almost sour, edgy, foreign.
He pulls on the chain.
It swings, dangling loosely
from the overhead exposed bulb,
the cubicle coming alive with soft light.
From the white moon on the cutting block,
he shaves a paper-thin fragment
onto the clean, smoothed wood.

I turn in circles, wondering
how this space might trap me.
My father's touch retrieves me.
The other hand barely taps
the carefully trimmed mustache.
The usually clear brown eyes drift
away, savoring remembered pleasures.
One hand still on my shoulder, he requests
another sample, which he passes on to me
in that strong, beautiful hand of a surgeon,
a hand supple as any dancing god's,
eternal as any Michelangelo.

We smile at one another, knowing
this aftertaste of cheese will be our excuse
for one last *café au lait* down the street.

The man cuts string with scissors
and then pulls it through the cheese,
first through the death-white skin,
then through the softer inner body.

In the outer room again,
newspapers folding, money,
a few olives, cash-register bell,
my father asks about the old people.
The man seems to know me for the first time,
like old friends going home in the dark,
tired from a hard day in the cane fields,
sharing their dreams of escape west
into those nearby sawmill towns
scattered in the wild longleaf pines.

The man smiles, perhaps remembers
some child in the Old Country, waiting
with respect for his words to count,
or maybe the man smiles at my father,
to whom my opinion already matters.
Maybe he's just glad to sell cheese,
this rare business in an echoing room.
A fly would have sounded like a bomber,
but there are no flies inside
though the Quarter is full of
urined beer, garbage perfumes
of horse, coffee, and fish,
the yeasty smell of the brewery.
Nothing penetrates the cleanliness
and sweet darkness of this store,
occasional mote of dust passing,
almost suspended in the silence.

Wood wears smooth, and
memories age like cheese.
In the warehouse of memory,
the dead are alive and waiting,
their laughter rumbling faintly
like a party a mile away.
Today the door is locked.
Old customers knock, and

sometimes, someone answers,
but the street intrudes,
despite boarded windows.
Cars sit, bumper to bumper,
fumes crossing every doorway.
There is no longer the smell of yeast
because the brewery has moved.

The Swan Room, 1957

Monteleone Hotel, New Orleans

The doors swing open,
walls painted with swans.
Waiters lift silver domes from bone
china on the starched tablecloth.

Between the brown crust of brabant potatoes
and the taut green lace of parsley,
my knife slices into the rare prime rib —
pink, moist, and firm.

A tuxedoed combo muffles
the clinking forks and ice cubes.
Couples shuffle the dance floor,
food and wine abandoned,
while they sniff
each other's hair.

After cheesecake Daddy pays,
then introduces us to the marimbist,
friend long before we were born.

I can still taste the sugar
when we take the elevator to our room,
pretending I'm grown up as I slip
into pajamas in the bright bathroom
and brush my teeth, grinning
at the boy in the mirror.
Then I go to bed, pull up
the covers and snuggle
under cold sheets,
wide awake.

The Photographer, Wrestling with Words

for Holly Wright

She rubs thumb across fingertips,
as if in examining exquisite silk,
she finds it turns into air.

From the screen her mother stares,
a large image immersed in black water,
head thrown back, emerging.

The slide show continues, slicing darkness,
a woman's face hidden by defiant fist
raised against the camera's evil eye.

The voice invites me to pull down the fist,
to see into and beyond the self-portrait,
to enter the projectionist's beam,

but I am entering unidentifiable landscapes,
hands transformed into sand dunes and caves,
slide after slide, the universe sliding.

Lingering at an image of giant fingers
offering a silky, almost invisible lens,
the photographer grapples for a term:

"The unpalpability of images," she says,
rubbing fingers again in darkness.
"We grasp at what dissolves.

"Photographers shouldn't try to capture.
The best subject drops the mask freely
and invites us to see beneath the hide."

Slide after slide, her photographs speak,
reawakening what already lives within me,
memories waiting to be accepted as gifts.

At home a small, slightly blurred but perfect
black and white of my father long dead
rests, framed in silver on my desk:

Taken in Panama in his white suit,
beside three faceless black girls
clutching themselves like three graces.

Overhead the sign, *Prohibido el transito
de carros*. He casually dangles a camera
in one hand, the young summer intern

assigned to healing steamship passengers
for the United Fruit Company. He smiles
with this first taste of the world.

Never until this darkened auditorium
have I wondered so about the photographer,
also no doubt now dust and air, yet

who still gives back fresh at any glance
that moment in which an intimate stranger
and my father and these graces consented.

Photographs of My Mother

1: Black and White

Mother is smiling, twenty-six or -seven.
She's watching something at the camera's right.
Her lips are parted.

At night the small white shells
from her earlobes will rest
on the mahogany dresser.
She will rub face cream
into the already smooth skin.

When Mother kisses me goodnight,
the clean, delicate scent of face cream
speaks of her happiness.

I am a little less than five
the day the photographs are made.
In my own I am smiling too.

2: Profession of Doubt

Mother, do you denounce dark rooms
and what develops within?

Do you reject cameras
and the exposures of film?

Will you accept the positives
as well as the negatives?

Do you believe in subjects?
That you could be the subject of a poem?
Will you unwrap all objects?
Will you be the verbs
that you are born to be?

Will you trust
the child standing on her soap box,
intriguing the young medical student?

Will you accept the memories of sunlight?
That though your fair skin burned,
you stunned the Galveston beaches
in a blue-satin swimsuit?

3: The Other Photograph

You are standing beside a car.
Your sunglasses obscure the beauty
of your eyes, but it shines through
the smile. Your large black hat
is stylish. So are your dress
and shoes. Your feet do not hurt,
and you are going somewhere.
Your hand rests on the handle.
I have not yet been conceived.

4: We Are Having Another Day

You cry, recalling Fred's gifts,
those large arrangements of flowers,
taller than children and sweeter,
lasting about as long.

The doorbell rings. Open it.

The fragrance of surprise
is its own gift, you know.

The doorbell rings again
and again.

"She had her day," Fred said
of that oil painting he admired.
He sent you flowers until he died.

These small seashells on your dresser
contain worlds we cannot crack open.

Put them on again and smile,
and take them off at night,
apply the silky face cream,
and no matter what stands
at the camera's right, kiss
and say goodnight, smearing
the scent of this cream
transparent into our dreams.

My Sister and the Knives

Enticed by the new-house perfumes
of sawdust and fresh paint, we crawled
into the small, dark space intended
for the canister vacuum. Trapped
on the wrong side of its latched door,
we cried till Mother heard
and sprang the lock.

Days later the frisky dog raced
through the house and pinned you
to the polished wooden floor
beneath the dining table.
"He's eating me," you screamed.
His pink tongue licked your face.

Years later, confident, you sit,
a do-it-yourself repair-person,
every knife in the house glittering
before you on the table.

In your new craft, you saw away
with the sharpest you can find.
A cylindrical lamp-part yields,
dividing under your grind.

Your children stare, in awe.
They hold their breath, afraid
of some new slice.

You spread the remaining pieces
beneath your slender fingers,
amazed that you have fixed the lamp.
It shines. You smile. You turn it off
and on again to prove your point.

On the Birth and Death of My Sister's Son Jared

Going home without you,
we stare into the darkness,
our car speeding through the trees.
The womb of night stares back.

You have been with us, Jared,
in games or dreams, sometimes forgotten
while we played with other thoughts,
but you waited until now,
fragile thought, strong thought,
clear and bright as the morning
rolling out of your darkness
like the big glass blue eye of God,
rolling until you struck us in the face.

Morning light falls across Whiskey Chitta Creek,
a new sign proclaiming the ancient Indian name,
Ouiska Chitto, a creek as clear as whiskey,
a word the locals fear, like firewater,
words, transforming nothing.
The cold, smooth creek passes away,
uncontrollable and pure into the woods,
and August sunlight breaks through the trees,
morning light passing through spaces
we do not yet understand.

The last five miles into town are like home.
Coltharp's Auction Barn turns up on the curve.
Across the highway in the near pasture,
the black bull under the fruit tree sniffs the air,
his testicles swaying in the breeze, and beyond him,
in the far green field, chalk-white Charolais cattle
eat grass and talk about flies, dreaming, unaware
of the fate of their friends auctioned off every week.
They chew and dream and will not recognize us
even though we've passed this way for years.

A Brother's Ring

You missed it somewhere on the course,
between holes you were trying to sink,
the emptiness, the nakedness,
the noticed finger rarely bare
of our father's ring.

You take it off to sleep and bathe
and never will be parted with it
otherwise, except when you slip
it into a bag with watch
and wallet, stow it safely
until the game is over.

Last week, for the first time,
the bare finger spoke.
You opened the bag in fear
to emptiness, then in panic
left the game, retracing fairways,
asking all on the course
if they'd seen
a wide gold band
the large diamond
the two small ruby eyes.

You didn't say
it was Mother's anniversary
gift to him their twenty-fifth.

You asked everywhere,
fearing the irrecoverable,
knowing how easily money
can buy and how hard
some things that cannot
be bought back — you flew
on the course, into the club-
house, the manager reassuring
sometimes people turn in
the smallest objects.

You retraced the green, dejected,
when suddenly in the side grasses
a glittery circle of gold
a larger splash of white
and two red eyes.

The Burning Bush

You wanted her to see
the painting, but she
died too soon.

You were across the water.
The burning bush waited
on this side, its last
splash of living paint
swirled onto the canvas.

She beat us to it, anyway.
The canvas is alive,
pigments breaking apart.

Framed, wired, and hung,
over your bed this sign
will burn, and you will read
yourself to sleep
beneath its light.

Among Cherry Blossoms

for my sister Ann

Under cherry blossoms I picnic on the grass,
watching the sun sink into the Tidal Basin,
while I sip wine and eat spinach pie,
the horizon nibbling away
the sweetest moments.

Grandpa never saw cherry blossoms.
Whenever he called us his little flower garden,
I imagined roses of every color, bright daisies,
irises, here and there a tall gladiola,
and in the thick, lush green some wildness,
all surrounded by a gray or white fence.
The fences have fallen, Ann,
our full lives wild with flowers.

Did he foresee more of this world than Washington,
that first glimpse beyond his beautiful, volatile island
north in the cavalry warring past industrialized Milan?
Later, worn, returning home, down through the sole
of his torn country, he chose to sell everything,
and abandoning grief he sailed from Palermo
with parents and sister and her orphaned children.
They entrusted their island to the wind
and then looked back only once.

In the New World he wandered New York for days,
searching in the wrong language for the houses
of brothers and friends who had gone before.
Eventually in a new south they built homes
and planted gardens and fig trees, now old.
Four of those six are buried there.
The only one left still
faithfully tends her garden
and sends me gifts of dried oregano,
mint, and *basilico*, perfumed bags
as exotic as frankincense, magic
for the sauces of our family's past.
I eat pasta and I think of her.
What is it like to be the last?

Sister, we can't think of one another dead,
but if you are the one who lasts longer,
I hope you'll revisit this memorial
and remember in the shimmering world
that we have laughed together.

There were no blossoms
that hot summer day years ago
when we climbed the white steps,
unimpressed by old bronze Jefferson
but happy to play in his shade,
laughing at our powerful echoes.

Under the dome children still explore
their shadows with the latest cameras,
but now the blossoms have arrived,
small dancing shadows across marble.
I don't remember so much water.
If the world is supposed to shrink,
for some reason, this one hasn't.

Things happen.
We grow old in different cities,
our lives filling to the brim.
We didn't foresee the hard miles,
the wrinkled years and scarred hearts,
maps creased and refolded into fringe,

or the joy of the longed-for and found,
like a brother's home in a new city or
the enjoyable conclusions that keep sending us
back to their beginnings for more. Or elsewhere,
old immigration papers in strange, flowery script,
a heavy silver chain without its watch, and
in the yellowed Italian prayerbook, a faded shamrock,
which, rediscovered, rekindles light among holy words.

RELATIVES AND FRIENDS

La casa nun s'acchiana senza scala.
— Antonio Veneziano

Snow Goose

for an uncle on the night of his laying out

Trying to fall asleep
under the outstretched wings
of the stuffed white goose
in my Aunt Bea's game room
in Lake Charles, Louisiana,
I can't put you from my mind.

I am dead-tired,
and in the darkness
the black eyes of the goose
stare me down,
mouth wired shut, wings spread,
separated from the freezing reality
of Canadian skies.

To bring on sleep
and dispel this face-to-face contest
(the goose will not look away), I talk to you,
closing my eyes and pretending I am the dead man,
cold like you, dressed in a suit, rosary in hand.

After a while, an explosion wakes me.
A blood vessel popping in my brain?
Or a car backfiring in the alley?
The white face of the goose
hangs over me, smiling blankly,
wings extended, about to beat the air.

You are laid in your coffin,
no shoes, no billfold, and
one of your fingers hangs in the air,
refusing to lie down, extended, instead,
slightly over the surface of your coat,
stiff, as if about to select another bead.
The muscles of your arm will not let you rest,
your wings fixed, your stillness
like the sound of my breathing
in this room.

I continue to wait,
and the longer I have to wait,
the more I learn about waiting,
the less anxiety I have about
going to sleep, though the waiting
only increases my longing for the sleep
that rushes in with new dreams like flight
into these old bodies.

PM and the Snow-Cone Stand

Ha! What flavor you want?
A man always knows what he wants.
You're a man when you're one and twenty.
When I came to this country,
your grandpa took me
into that wooden building
and told me
it was mine.

"Uncle," I replied,
"I will never forget
your kindness."

"This is not kindness,"
he said. "You are my
brother's son. I do
what I can do."

Years later, behind that store,
in the house where I still try
to live, my wife died. I swear
to God, she hated guns. I will
never understand.

Do you remember how she'd laugh,
shaking till she had to dab
her eyes with the handkerchief?

Do you like cherry
or pineapple?
Lemon-lime?
I can make you
a rainbow.

Put your money away.
Your father was my cousin,
but he was like my brother.
Whatever PM can do for you,
PM will do.

Times Your Aunt Mary Needs You

You're feasting on crawfish jambalaya
at a beautiful woman's house across town
when your Aunt Mary calls for help.
A truck has driven into
her dining-room wall.

Another time she calls
because her oven timer
won't turn off. The bell
nearly drives you both crazy
until the electrician arrives
to kill it, grinning.

Later, in another city, you wait
stranded in her new living room
while someone reattaches your rearview.
She's so relieved you're here because
today suddenly after all these years
her oven won't turn off.

Not the bell, but those coils,
getting hotter and hotter,
hotter than you ever expected
to cook in your old ages.

The Olive-Oil Can

Brother and Sister and Brother and Sister and Brother
all got their portions from the same big can.
Aunt Bennie would get it shipped freight
to her, then call them separately.
They'd come with their empty cans,
get their fill. Then she would
show them the price, written in pencil
on a short piece of white paper.
They would write her a check
or give her cash.

The rates of use might have varied,
but everyone would be ready
when the shipment arrived —

something about balance.

Visiting My Cousin

Sitting at the front window,
he's watching the blackbirds
fluttering in the neighbor's trees.
He's a Down's syndrome victim, and
although he's graying prematurely,
this isn't exactly a deathwatch.

I don't know that
he sees his mother come in,
a finger raised to her lips.
The room is still full of her perfume.
Months after the funeral, he told me
he wanted to dig her up.

Now, sitting in his living room,
he turns around to smile at me.
"The birds are happy," he says.
Then he faces the window again
in his favorite chair,
his back to me.

Hydrangea

We dangled legs from the high porch.
My cousins used words I didn't comprehend.
Inside, Nonna continued to die.
She'd been dying all my life,
confined to bed.

I did not even know why
my cousins laughed at me.
I jumped from the porch
into the flowers, picked up
a crushed blue hydrangea blossom
and held it gently in my lap.

Then I raised it high into the air
above my head, and like the priest
with the white host at Mass, I sang,
"Hocus pocus, God is here."
They said I'd go to hell.

I ran inside
and placed it in her
thin, white hands.

She blessed me
in the language
I understood.

The Grocer

He lost his wife years ago to diabetes,
somewhere under the counter
or behind the store.

One minute he was cutting T-bones,
the next he was a widower.
The widows rushed in, as usual,
but he was too fast, or slow.

He courted them all with gifts
but slept alone for the next
twenty years. What a waste,
of good produce, they used to say.

Rocky and Mary Time

Christmases they called from New York,
persistent enough to get through the jam
with their annual wishes,
faces I'd never seen
except in old, sixteen-millimeter,
brightly colored film exposed
before I'd been conceived:

Clowning, the young soldier encircles
his bride's waist from behind,
presses his face against hers, nuzzles,
and lifts her against his stomach,
her feet off the ground. Nearby
my mother, laughing, is drawn
into their arms. A shadow rises
beneath their feet, my father,
the cameraman, for whom they dance
and play.

Years later they no longer call.
Has our name been scratched from their book,
pencilled out neatly, perhaps, or x-ed
with ink? Or have they too passed
into some other silent footage?

Good Wine Wasted and a Place to Rest

an elegy for Tony Manino at 42

Dark wine splattered on the street,
wasted among the broken green glass,
in my arms the split and empty paper bag.
People crossed to the other side fast,
the light about to change.

The next day two green fragments remained,
embedded like emerald eyes in the manhole cover,
no trace of the good Bardolino I'd intended
to christen my new home with.

Miles away you were dying too soon,
always too soon, we say. Knock, knock.
Who's there? Go away. No room here.

I remember the light in your eyes.
As boys we lit candles at the same altar,
learning to hand the cruets and ring bells,
trying out our first Latin responses.
After Mass, discarding the white surplices
and stripped down to black cassocks,
we could almost be boys again.

Every March 19, white-robed children approached
the candlelit saint standing on the table,
surrounded by flowers and the rare breads,
the sugary *sfingi*, the fig cakes, the clustered *pignolata*,
or the clove-scented, teeth-breaking Dead Men's Bones
and other such sweet delicacies for the mid-Lenten
feast minus meat and cheese, but with tangy breadcrumbs
sprinkled instead on the *pasta con sarde*, the bread-
stuffed artichokes, greens, and *carduni* rubbed fragment
with olive oil, fish like *baccalà* dressed and
hand-painted with delicious make-up, creations
unimaginable, and for every guest a dried fava bean,
blessed, to be taken home against ill fates.
You hosted your family's celebration, opening
the doors and retelling the ancient stories.
"Remember their struggle," you said, smiling.

The saints stood at the door, waiting.
Knock, knock. Who's there? Go away.
Inside an old woman scratched her head to recall
the traditional dialogue, in time the Dialect lost
or muffled. Knock, knock. Who's there?

"*Santi!* The Holy Saints!" the children answered.
The door opened, the food blessed, and only after
the saints did we follow and eat, feasting
and thanking our patron, St. Joseph,
but the abundance was always saved
to be taken to the unforgotten poor.

In the hungry eyes of the world's streets,
I see you appearing and disappearing,
a flickering light, an older saint.
In the changing unsteadied hum of time,
people go on to some other sameness,
except for your wife and children.
Now someone else must tell the story
of the long, hungry search, the emptiness,
the doors we try, waiting. Knock, knock.
Go away, the voices on the other side insist,
but we keep knocking until at last a door opens
and someone says, "Yes, come in.
There is food for everyone."

Remembering the *Titanic* Every April 15

for Sultana Harreck, a survivor

Remember us, the voices sang.
The life rafts drifted. "Nearer, My God,
to Thee." The big ship tilted
and was gone.

Whatever Sultana saw
remained in her heart.
She never cursed the ice
or the cracked hull
that blessed her immigration.

For years disc jockeys phoned
to ease their tense listeners
through the big tax deadline.
The happy coincidence was
no happy anniversary.
She accepted their wishes
but never tossed confetti.

For years she sat, confined, a witness
at the living-room, plate-glass window,
in the wheelchair that did not roll far.
Her babies grew old, and one died stung.
A bee sting, Mother Harreck cried.

Perhaps there'd been no bee, no sting,
but a child's deep pain carried too long,
the edge growing sharper in secret until at last

other voices, older, cutting into darkest oceans, called,
Remember the ice and remember us who drift
awhile, then watch hard and long
at our plate-glass windows, waiting
for we all know what.

Silver Dimes, Newly Minted, 1992

for Gladys, d. 1967

I subtract the numbers
and the silver appears,
like a strand of hair.

How did it get so long?
Did the single strand
turn at once, a unified
shiver, a black line
blanching iridescent,

the line crossed,
like the cross hairs
in a rifle's sight?

Twenty-five years call for silver,
not the kind you can
sink teeth into,

not the lining of the sky,
not clouds,
not coins.

STUDENTS IN WORLDS
THAT NO LONGER EXIST

. . . a pause has fallen between us like a petal.
— Vassar Miller

The Evening News

With every death I search the boxes
for letters, photographs, anything
to refute the obliteration of flesh,
some proof that blood has flowed
and heart beaten. Last year
at this time, whole countries
existed that are no more.

I watch the news for the names,
fragments that have become
something else. To scissor the maps
into blues and yellows and pinks
would only make more chaos.
I cannot name the pieces
of this aftermath.
It is still the world
but not the world I know.

Local Peaches

Beside the hand-painted sign,
a young Mennonite woman sits,
black-skull-capped
head buried
in a book,

long, black-stockinged legs dangling
from the wagon loaded with peaches
waiting to be rubbed,
squeezed, eaten.

Curves

for Martha

The back road is naked now
where my black roadster
used to shoot around and up
my hilly curve through pine trees.
Like the adolescent thrills and my Jag,
the stand of pines is gone.

Miles down the road your curve waits.
Coming home from a night wedding,
a bridesmaid dress in the trunk,
the car shattered into the ditch,
your father dead, you paralyzed,
the nearby gas station demolished,
and the other car.

On this curve, as in the senior-yearbook ad,
you always appear, not in the real wheelchair
but as a lingering image in the black leotards
I'd seen you in two days before the wreck,
leaning against the dance bar, a student
whose head the photographer was turning
to hide the loss of an earring.
The studio mirror on the back wall
was an accidental witness.
It saw why you were smiling.

In another yearbook ad,
you grin, pointing a butcher knife
into a slab of fatty beef,
four pounds of meat
on the scale behind.
What's the photographer said?
Come on, cheerleader.
Give us a T-bone.
Give us a loin.
Give us a rib-tickling
slice down the middle.
You didn't suspect
that for years you'd be rolled out
onto the cinder track at ball games,
alumna wheelchair-cheerleader,
learning again to talk.

When I spoke to you
for the first time in years,
I didn't know you were about to be
confined to the nursing home, and
when I called out "Pee Wee,"
I realized how far off I was, and
my knees went weak under your gaze,
and when I told you who I was,
you smiled out of your steel walker,
making me feel like a ballerina
caught between positions,
forgetting what comes
next —

I went home last week, and
the treeless field angered me.
For years I've presumed to know you,
but truth comes up over me
a few miles late, down the road,
a wildcat I almost hit.

Life is fast
even without a Jag.
The ditch is now filled in.
Even the gas station ruins are gone.
But despite whatever else
appears or disappears here,
our curves will always
be as much our own
as our names.

Parade Ground

A walk at night through the parade ground,
the occasional laughter of strangers,
headlights leaving long streaks on the night,
a red traffic light changing to green,
the soft cushion of earth under my feet,
I am walking on a bed.

Later, at two in the morning,
there are no people,
and the lights are farther apart.
The only sound is the chain on the flagpole,
clanging like faraway electronic music.
A stray truck passes in the street.

The clouds break apart,
dissolving into black sky.
There are no stars, no light
except the widely spaced streetlamps,
white spheres, like the heads
of armless gray guards,
glowing facelessly.

Crossing the empty parade ground,
I am approaching the campanile,
the tall clock-faced tower
that stands firm,
forever erect,
chiming
quarter-hours.

How can a man
stay up like this —
awake when everyone else
is asleep? Wouldn't dreams
be easier than walking?
Insomniac's fantasy.

Reaching the tower,
I lean against the wall,
surveying the open space,
the Greek Revival law school before me,
and broken landscapes adjacent,
trees, buildings, portals

without doors,
sidewalks
circulating
like treadmills.

I am thinking about
placing my body
in the middle of the field,
throwing myself down
and going to sleep,
but a blue light on the street,
a police car chasing a speeder,
reminds me of the night patrol,
the security guards who sneak around
in search of peeking toms
and other perverts.
How would I explain
that I was sleepless
until at last I found
the best spot
to close my eyes?

I give up
and walk home
for coffee and a book
until the sun comes up,
when I shower and go, bleary-eyed,
to class, the fast slow-pace
of being half-awake.

Crossing the parade ground
in the morning rush of light
and students on their casual ways,
I see a student, carrying her books,
dropping cigarette ashes.
I almost stop her
with my request
not to burn my sheets,
but at the far end of the field,
I see the Air Force Rifle Corps
marching in place, about to take off.
I hurry on my way, silently,
to avoid the invasion.

Villanelle on the Suicide of a Young Belgian Teacher Soon to Be Naturalized

Truth is not merchandise.
— Meister Eckhart

Children over 40 inches pay full fare,
but truth is neither relief nor merchandise.
What did you think you were buying, Jean-Pierre?

You buy relief with laughter or a gun, swear
those obscene Belgian curses, or theorize,
"Children over 40 inches pay full fare."

Your violence is unanswerable despair.
You have taken leave without paying goodbyes.
What did you think you were buying, Jean-Pierre?

A piano? Passport? Eternal youth? We bear
the judgment of those who do not realize
children over 40 inches pay full fare.

Mercy cannot be bought, and yet your unfair
silence buys our mercy, unmerited prize.
What did you think you were buying Jean-Pierre?

You teach us more than French and music. You stare
behind your smiles, blood-soaked, and your laughter dies.
Children over 40 inches pay full fare.
What did you think you were buying, Jean-Pierre?

William Faulkner, Sacred Cow

Every grave is worth dancing on.
I wouldn't be offended by wild pigs
rooting around mine for spare ribs, or
if my feet stick up out of the dirt,
occasional birds picking wild berries
from between my toes.

I didn't come as a death-pilgrim
to read the scribblings on your study wall
but to dance through your woods like a squirrel
scampering after ghost-words, the nuts
of another generation.

Fortunately your house was locked,
so I wasn't tempted to sit
behind your desk or upon your toilet
or lie down upon your bed. At your grave
when I found rowan acorns budding
pale green shoots instead of your bones,
I laughed, hoping we're alike
inside these different skins.

I'd like to be like you, Bill,
a solitary old squirrel-chaser
with my own woods to hide in
and walls to write on, but I'd be
an embarrassed sacred cow,
every indiscretion a national landmark,
turds bronzed, photos enlarged
to reveal stray whiskers or
whether I dressed right or left.

But I make a poor golden calf
with the liabilities of a metal ego.
Whatever success I order —
fame, money, women, humility
— I remain the bellowing male beast
at the center of the field, full
of my own sound and fury, so full
of bull that I sometimes forget
that I also smell like cow.

We ought to be ashamed to sanctify
ourselves in life, turn our words into milk
which we pray the world will suck for,
to imagine our T-bone and ground-round bodies
dressed into Veal Oscar or Beef Wellington.

But I'd be proud to wag bells
along your cow trail through the woods,
late in the evening, a worn path
dotted with patties or mushrooms,
a gentle, ghostly trudging homeward
to be milked of whatever words
convey our private common jokes,
our joyful good grief.

Use the Common Present to Report What a Person or Thing Does Regularly (or Even the Mean Blue Jay Looking into the Window Cannot Lift the Awning but Drops, Fluttered Out, onto the Sidewalk, Hops Up Again, Escaping)

Like the trashman
on the back of the truck
pretending we haven't stared,
who turns away, gazing
at the blank curb,
sucking the universe
in through his cigarette,

when the light turns green
he stretches, leans, then,
uncrossing legs, springs

like a cat he scares
off the aluminum can,
dumps trash into
the city truck.

Even if I want
I can't pretend
we haven't stared.
No escaping the eye
once captured

(a child in a home movie,
floating the parade
in a white satin childhood,
beside a gold papier-mâché lion,
stares into eternity
unabashed, in full color,
waves to the camera
for years on this film,
not seeing what

the film won't forget —
repeating the wave,
at one moment, lips
part, no words, only

the soundless click
of the projector)

at the next block,
a red light and no cans,
the trashman composes him-
self on the ledge.
             I think,
if the truck starts too fast
he'll fall under my wheel.
          He looks
up, flinches to be trapped, no-
where to turn.
          When the light changes,
he tosses the stub, grenade-like.
          He is killing the mirror.
          He is meaner
          than I ever
          imagined.

Using the Common Future to Report What Will Happen Under Certain Conditions (or Is This One to Report What Will Occur Regardless of Human Intent?)

Someday rows of coins
stacked along the narrow ledge
of the black pay phone will mean
as little to you too.

You will lean against the wall,
considering this wealth of change,
knowing there's no right combination
of numbers to be bought.

Even if you close your eyes,
the dead receiver in your hand
will not speak.
            Those of us across town
will lift our wordless hands, waiting.
The yellow-tiled walls will remain clean,
the long, invisible floor spotless.
You will want to believe
that corridors of flesh exist.
But even if you force quarters
into the slot, supposing intimacy,
the music of coins, like metal bones,
clinking as they fall into the box,
will catch desperately.

Even when no one answers
and the dimes and
nickels tumble back
and the quarters,

the same quarters,
the same faces,
all the same things
you started out with,
come back,

you suppose everything else
will come back too,
becoming the same,
coming back.

The Music of Helen Keller's Hands

an elegy for Joy Scantlebury,
poet, student, and friend

1

The high-ceilinged New Orleans sun porch
was covered with hanging cement-baskets,
a profusion of sunlit ferns, draping
long, green, delicate fingers from overhead.

In the large wicker chair, she sat
in gray lawn dress and large hat,
she too a visitor to the stately
home of Colonel and Mrs. Edmonds.
You and your twin sister had come
from down the block of Audubon Boulevard,
where your nurse and maid and parents
had prepared you for the great woman's
hands upon your little faces.

Did the hands that touched your face
anoint your poet's voice?

2

With death, I feared I'd lost your voice,
resting in its mylar-thin brown tape
within the brief cassette you'd made for me.

I've searched my house for this recording
in the way I sometimes search for letters,
photographs, or silver rings — mementos
that somehow prove our recently dead
have lived: your poems, your voice,
ten minutes' worth you'd read into the tape.
But lost? Into what wooden crag
have you been lodged?
Into what empty pocket
have you slipped?

3

My own first words have vanished too,
chipped and worn away out of the
black grooves of the primitive disk
my parents paid for.

"Where are you going?"
the voices asked.

"To Beaunut," I said.
I was always going
to Texas.

For twenty-five cents
on a painted horse
outside the grocery store,
I was always racing
toward a line I didn't
know was close.

Over and over my small answer
rose out of the black coating
of that metal record. With wear
it chipped and flaked into
the silvery plate beneath.

I listened as the voices disappeared,
until at last the chips had opened
so much space no voice could
bridge the silver chasms.

4

Your poems are silver chasms too,
yet out of them comes back your voice,
freed from page, not lost at all.

It echoes in a darkening auditorium
where houselights are going out.
On stage a great woman appears,
contralto-like, about to sing,
but opening her arms to the silence,
she extends her hands into empty air,
toward the faces of children
waiting to be touched.

Resurrection Scherzo

Three cars struck.
He must have bounced back and up
like a pinball on that street he'd walked
for twenty years in broken shoes,
the headlights cracking in the dark.
The next day's news camera avoided
the body but lingered on the isolated,
doubly crushed shoe.

I heard the news later, across
sautéed crawfish and swirls of
frenetic violins, unidentifiably
familiar, whirling around with
sounds we'd already heard in the
swollen glasses of white wine.

He died going home hungry,
not even a drink, but empty,
except for the cook's good words
shared as a last meal
a thousand feet from death.

On campus the empty office waited:
neat stacks of final essays,
files cleaner than the past,
unusual except as casual other facts
of the day's official resignation.

Over the coffin the priest denied
coincidence, praised the blessing
of being struck down when
there's nowhere else to go.
Even those not crying knew
Monsignor was right.
We get what we need.

Christ, the violence of a scherzo
recognized months later, Beethoven,
the movements of such last music
we live and die in — Christ,
how we want to rise out of it
in new shoes and straightened backs.

We step, breathing out our blood
scherzo, relieved by what cannot be
accident, but struck by the familiar
percussion of our streets, the inevitable
resolution of particular
private harmonies.

Boxes of Books

We dream of shelves
upon which one day
our spines might rest,
not crowded back to back
in damp cardboard
aching with the subtleties
of mildew.

We dream of polished wood
and of thick, clean glass
sliding open on brass hinges
and of hands turning the pages
once again allowing the words
to breathe.

LOVE LESSONS

. . . in one luminous second
we outmatched the cold.
— Joy Scantlebury

The Infinite Possibilities of Desire

A hard fist pounds
against my plate-
glass brain.

Blood throbs.
A long wrinkle
creases down the side
of my face.

Why so late
in the cold evening
this impossiblity?

Your hand reaches
into my heart
and squeezes.

Ribs no longer
contain me.

"E lucevan le stelle"

He died last night on television.
Though he dies every third act,
eventually Cavaradossi outlives us.

The first time we heard him,
we were in the auditorium-heaven,
leaning forward into the darkness
like adolescents undressing shyly.
We knew the libretto even though
we weren't the stars yet.

The story doesn't change:
Tosca is deceived.
Cavaradossi is shot.
The theme rises in the finale
as Tosca leaps to her death.
We went out afterwards to eat
and celebrate our introduction
to live opera.

Last night, with my shoes off,
I smiled at the fate of lovers.
Nothing changes except the audience.
But I'm always stunned in Act Three
when that aria takes my breath away.

He sings a melody as beautiful as life.
Are you laughing at my corn, Tosca?
Miles away you cry like me,
not because of tragic endings
but because the joyful melody
wrenches deep into our lives
with the hard truth of its beauty.
Its eternal life is more certain
than the best videotapes.

Are you laughing, Tosca?
When I lean over too far,
stars fall out of the balcony.

Introductions and Mr. Kundalini

Your husband filled me with gin and feta
before we sat down to my first turkey curry,
first evening to know either of you
or California fifteen years ago.

I confessed I didn't know the Sufis.
"Then of course," you explained,
"you wouldn't know the Kundalini."

I'd known the names via books.
They'd always sounded like relatives or
someone's cousins I was supposed to know,
the Messinas, the Terracinas, the Timpas,
the Kundalinis.

(Mr. Kundalini knocks on the door,
a tiny retired grocer with a white mustache,
grows *cuccuzzu* and *finocchiu* and *escarola*,
which he gives away as gifts.)

The turkey curry we topped with pistachios
and raisins. I was in heaven until
you disappeared into the next room,
coming back in a flash with
a small enamelled-pastry serpent.

"This is only a representation,"
you confided across the candlelit table.
"Perhaps someday you will know the real
Kundalini. It uncoils suddenly, surges
up out of the dark, mysterious cage
at the base of the spine, springing
through sex, navel, heart, throat, head —"

Hot with gin and deep into the wine, I flushed,
"Ever heard of the *scardulini*?" I asked,
trying to counter with my own mysteries.
"Dead Men's Bones, a candy of the *siciliani*.
On a flattened brown, clove-scented lattice
is stuck a chalk-white bone so hard
it breaks teeth."

I turned the kundalini over in my hand,
blushing like a man caught examining
his penis at table.

You smiled at your husband.
He was clearing for the next course.
"*Dolci*, everyone?" he said, laughing
on his way out.

Her Wallpaper

for Judy Kahn

We rip wallpaper from the wood.
Our fingernails pick and tear
at the layers of strangers' lives.

The hammer I carry
grows lighter by the hour,
tighter in the grip of every year.
The green plants grip the wall,
which puckers as they grow
heavy with leaves and nails,
a living curtain through which
sunlight breaks.

The past is also a heavy curtain.
I want you to draw it back.
Sometimes it comes
so easily.

Someone in my head pushes the piano
up against an adjacent wall.

Someone cuts his arm on purpose.
Memories bleed into one another.
Your husbands stand somewhere
behind you, asking to be
confirmed like dominoes.

I peel back another layer of paper.
The words cascade down into the air,
announcing slowly as tiny particles
the names of who we were
and who we want to be.

A Sonata of Things You'll Never Know

for a friend with cerebral palsy

1: *Allegro*

I pound your mother's concert grand
with thinning, out-of-practice arms,
pages of black notes remembered clearly,
yet the right hand slips, misses a quick turn,
falls shimmering *con brio* into the strong left.

2: *Adagio cantabile*

One of these same hands last week felt strong,
holding my aunt's hand as she babbled
on her deathbed, eyes closed.
At her name she pressed fingers
lightly into my palm, thanked me
for coming. Pray, she begged
and slipped again into delirium.

3: *Rondo con fuoco*

This morning, I watched you twist hard
in recovery, your mother's arms curled about.
Only five years old, you try to cover the white-
blond hair cropped short from today's surgery,
the yellow question mark painted down your head.
Because the tube in your brain remains occluded,
someday you will endure other procedures.
Your mother struggles to comfort
but you thrash and cry anyway.
She will remember how your hand
struck out unknowingly against her neck,
one of those things no one can understand,
they say, unless you are a mother.

Animal Control

For days, actually nights,
I was awakened by the scratching
in my bedroom wall, a regular
3 a.m. alarm. I have a rat,
I told my landlord. "It can't
get in," he said, "except through
that attic trap over your stove."

But I heard the flopping, thundering romp
through the attic. Squirrels and raccoons,
I feared. Neighbors told stories.
I couldn't sleep enough
to have bad dreams.

My landlord laughed and gave me
rat poison. I opened the trap door
bravely.

The next night's noise was stranger,
again the next, as the fury eased
and my torturer weakened, its scratching
pared down to a lethargic scrape.

Then the silence of Holy Week.
After Easter a visitor's questions
brought back a childhood memory,
a Chrysler almost ruined
by an unfound egg.

No, the garbage was collected,
and the stench grew stronger.
There's something dead, I told
the landlord. He laughed until
a few days later in my backyard
he got a whiff.

By then my house was uninhabitable.
I drove up one evening to hear
my landlord's good news. "I called
Animal Control," he said,
pleased to report
he'd watched them pull
the dead possum from
under my home.

I've learned sometimes Animal Control
comes out with cages and carts away
the pests, live, but for some
destiny I don't ask about.

Now at night when I see a possum
cross the road, I cringe.

I'm glad my bedroom walls are silent,
but if the scratching returns next spring,
I will not put out rat poison.
I will call those who work more quickly.
I will trust in cages.

The Behavior of Ants

"Ants Behead Queen"
— Washington Post

The ants beheaded their queen.
She was riding their shoulders
when her regally big head stuck
in the new doorway.

None of her subjects noticed.
They enthroned her,
brought sugary platters.
No one could understand
why she'd lost
her appetite.

The *Post* reported the accident.
The zoo had to junk its colony
and start all over.

My kitchen is not such a zoo,
though a colony thrives.
Ants are dancing in my sink.
I have cleared my pantry
more than once, but
their samba continues.
My refrigerator is jammed
with exiled canisters.

I have sprayed poison, I confess,
until my throat turned red,
wiped thresholds with bleach
to repel the dotted lines
of invaders.

But they reappear near the faucet,
in the sink, in seams of windows.

I cannot make a cake.
I cannot let a baked chicken cool.

They approach my coffee cup.
I press them to quick deaths
beneath my fingers.

I sprinkle drops of lemon
on the windowsills,
lay lemon rinds
as casement guardians.

Nothing daunts these soldiers.
This morning in the war ruins,
I found them, wandering still
the formica desert, and on top
the acidic yellow dune,
a brave new creature,
a newly mutated species, I thought,
intended to survive all tactics,
waved a leg out of its head,
some strange new dance step
against the war with humans.

But I was wrong.
The soldier was carrying the still-
fighting remains of a comrade.
I pressed them both to death
into the lemony pulp.

I do not think ants think,
but afterwards, tempted to sniff
at this death hand, I wondered
how they felt crushed into
the bitter lemony pulp
and if it makes much difference
that the last fingers that press us
to death taste of the salt
that is human skin.

The Loop, Chincoteague, Virginia

for Deborah George

"This is how it was when it all began."

Your words seem lost in the August evening.
An egret lifts one leg, then another.
Beyond, on the wide, flat water,
another moves, a black egret, not a shadow,
but an identical creature, built the same,
moves the same. The only difference
is the darkness of its plumage.

The sun is going down, unseen,
hidden behind the almost unseen clouds.
It is that fragile time of day
when the light breaks the water,
turns gold or red or blue.
This evening, without the strong light,
the flat sheet of water pales gray.
The egrets lift themselves out of it.
Another bird, larger, with streaked feathers,
skims the surface, tasting
whatever breeds there.

We sit in the car, comparing this moment
with others. The state in its wisdom
has separated this three-and-a-half mile
loop of water, grass, and road.
The sounds of our breathing remind
us of our other lives. We are not
really as we were
when it all began.

Tears and wild grasses and paved roads
call to us in this breathing.
As we start the car and leave,
we find some of the wild ponies
nibbling grasses. Legend has it,
they have descended from escaped cargo,
a Spanish galleon centuries ago.

"How hard to be a pregnant horse," you say.
I can see the animal's side bolt and quiver.
The belly hangs low, solid as a sack of flour.
The wind blows through her hair.

We cannot touch them.
Like the egrets, they are beyond us,
and we drive away, so close
to the world's beginning,
so far away from our own.

Cheese Graters

Rub the piece of metal against the cheese.
Or more easily, rub the piece of cheese
against the metal. Watch for scrapings.

If they fall into the bowl like pieces
of tiny fish-flesh, you will know
that you are grating well.

If you see nothing in the dish,
perhaps your cheese is too old
and too hard.

On the other hand,
it may only portend
bifocals.

A Yard Full of Sunken People

The car, backing up into the front yard, sinks
into the new mud. The harder we try,
the deeper our wheels sink, spitting
out earth as the tires spin,
the green turf dividing.

The car whirs, like a toy
out of water, paddling nowhere fast,
though if the treads chanced to catch,
there'd be no catching it,

like the bull in the china shop,
obliterating every gift in sight,
even fragile borders we'd not considered,
plate-glass windows and double doors,
the bifocaled clerk, the coffee cup
on the counter, the counter itself,
everything, everyone sinking,
spinning —
                    and then afterwards,
the immense relief, when the tow
truck leaves and the car rests,
purring on the concrete driveway,
waiting to go, daring anyone
to make another false move.

The Swimming Teacher

You gave me that first confidence.
Against my fear of the big, cold volume
of water, we overcame by your outstretched
arms and the wriggly wavy lines
of your body beneath the surface.

You were like Ava Gardner to me.
Something stirred inside
I couldn't name.

I wanted to jump,
but I didn't know
what would happen
when I crashed through
the cold, blue-green sheet,
the swimming-pool surface
in which your warmth waited
and coaxed me to leap.

Don't hesitate, you said.
I leaped, and with every leap
the excitement increased.

And now sometimes when I leap
knowing full well the cold volume,
I still want to take that dare
because I know someone
like you or Ava Gardner
might be waiting,

and even if there's not,
I know, as you have taught,
the water will not let
me drown. So I leap

and look for
outstretched arms,
and I jump.
I jump.
I jump.

Fireflies and the Dry Cleaners

I guess I'd sneer too
if dirty clothes were thrown at me all day,
armpit perspiration, crotch and ketchup stains.

We wrangled over tuxedo buttons
she'd ironed off their first cleaning.
"Cheap," she said, "you've got to complain.
Stop the world from making cheap buttons."
She held the pieces in her hand as proof,
plastic fragments of some tiny universe.

Tonight, on my way home from night-class,
fireflies rose up out of an open yard,
their green bodies turning off and on
against the deep blue darkness.
Later, miles closer to my front door,
a single green dot pulsed hello.

Relish this evening's light,
its signal seemed to translate,
no stain of moonlight,
no sneering entrepreneur.

Enjoy the light of now, it said,
for when you find yourself stripped
down to the robe of the future
you have already been wearing,
there will be no need to pay,

and life's perfumes will rise,
glowing their incensed embers
and pulsing like fireflies
in the widening night
that will send dry
cleaners eternally
out of business.

The Man Who Picked Up Nails

There was a man who picked up nails. He walked around with a small beast inside him. Sometimes it looked like a miniature bear. He would cradle the bear, and it would snarl and pretend that it wasn't a bear. But they both knew what it was. Somehow or other, the man figured that the bear was connected with his habit of picking up nails. He didn't think the bear ate the nails. It wasn't even that the bear called out or up to him to stop on the street whenever he saw one of those nails in front of him. But he knew it was right to pick up nails and that if he didn't pick one up when he saw it, someone, maybe even he himself, might run over it, get a flat tire or a punctured foot. He'd had a tetanus booster, but still he didn't want to take a chance.

The History of Pain

Conceived in
one direction,
it comes out
another.
Its delivery
will be
consistent
with what
it will
be,
for laid
to rest
there will be
no rest
for the weary
will be
wearied out
with it
and the un-
wearied will al-
so be un-
wearied un-
to death.

Edward Hopper's *Cape Cod Morning*, 1950

She leans forward, hopeful, at the window,
waiting for the soothing stroke of love
to rise out of the dark forest
and brush away these inescapably
painful colors.

The colors purr, itching like a caged
animal as it rises out of sleep,
nervously trying to scratch
the bright, intangible sky.

The moment seems calm, and even
the full breasts hang caressed
in the rose dress, almost the flesh
of lips. The hopeful brow rises.
No glass pane obscures.

She waits, exposed in the bright light
of this moment, her arms and face
bare to it. Even the outer wall
glares under the hard scrutiny
of white paint.

She leans forward, hungry, at this window,
unsure if a wild beast or gentle lover
will answer in the breeze. Is it you?
she asks. Wait, it whispers, not yet,
my love. Wait.

Waiting at the Café du Monde, New Orleans

I wait for you at the Café du Monde.
Nearby a newspaper rustles, coins jingle
onto tabletops, tourists chatter, blurring
into old regulars, a pencil taps
a hard crossword.

Across Jackson Square a woman appears
on the balcony where Jenny Lind once sang.
The old wrought-iron railing was designed
by Micela de Pontalba, Almonester's daughter.
Iron flowers curl into the letters A & P.
The baroness wasn't advertising groceries.

I remember from my history Micela de Pontalba
whimsically renovating French marble palaces,
snapping fingers, dropping men, dodging bullets,
rich enough to sneeze money and shuffle oceans.
In the famous portrait, she wears a silk dress
and over each ear, large snail-shells of hair.

Across from the red-brick Pontalba Apartments,
beneath the cathedral he built centuries ago,
Old Almonester stirs in his crypt, dreaming
up the woman on the balcony into his daughter.
Her perfumed finger rises slowly in the wind.

The woman returning my gaze looks down
where strolling tourists seduce air for time.
On the corner a vendor sells red carnations
to a young Vietnamese buying his bride a memory.
A jazz funeral drones in the unseen distance.
The heat of this music burns into the air,
and when the woman looks at me again,
the warmed air between us slowly rubs
her perfume down into my body, where
it turns me hard in a public place.

I sip my *café au lait*
in the crowded open-air Café du Monde.
A passing bus splashes oil. People move,
inching up the line for tables. Not much changes.
I miss the big silver bowls that used to be

chained to the dark wood and the thick glasses of
fish-scented water sliding across the marble counter,
powdered sugar from *beignets* melting
into wet smudges under real coins.

When you arrive and kiss me hello,
you smile, telling me how you once saw
right across the street, under the shadows
of the Pontalba Apartments, where the famous sleep,
a crazed young man charging through the crowd
like a huge, frightened bull, escaping
hard and obvious in his loose clothes.

Over your shoulder I see the woman
on the balcony watching, begging to be
released from the costly wrought iron.

We order more *café au lait*, grateful for
the sometimes easy temporariness of life,
when words don't seem to matter much
and love doesn't mind the wait.

LAST WORDS

The wind blows where it will.
— John 3:8

Drinking from a Paper Cup

In the days before manufactured paper cups,
Daddy showed me a way to fold a sheet
of paper into a hat or cup.

He could make a colored hat
from the Sunday funnies and
knight me with pointed newsprint
or red-bonnet my sisters
with leftover Christmas wrappings.

With expert surgeon fingers,
he could make tiny hats too
for canaries or robins,
though we had none.

Sometimes he filled these with tap water.
Other times he floated paper armadas
in the white enamel tub.

I found one of these relics.
It had never floated
or carried water to lips.
On blue and white prescription paper,
it had waited, folded years
past breath and thirst.

Yesterday by accident I began to fold
a street flier. T-shirt, bargains,
God knows what. A crease, then
another, like flattened wings,
triangle, folds — without
the least difficulty, it appeared,
a medium-sized hat, a paper cup.

Last night I placed it on my table, inverted,
a slightly off-balanced pyramid, and later,
in my dreams, I filled it with cool water
and raised it to my lips.

Eviction Notices

I am an emptied house.
People moving in and out
of me do not knock.
New tenants find the holes
where old faces have hung.
Sometimes they have used the nails
of a previous calendar or clock.
Often they putty up
what seem senseless
cavities.

My bare rooms echo
with neighborhood rumors.
The "murder house" across town cries.
Nearby, a balcony overlooking the lake
is most restless in a rainstorm.
These and other secrets unfurl
themselves on summer nights.

Places speak,
though we have no pink tongues.
Our roofs may leak,
foundations crack.

Tear away old wallpaper,
and you may find words
of a former occupant.

I am a place, I say.
If you do not know me,
knock on this door.

If I do not answer,
perhaps it is because
no one is home
anymore.

Lost: Paperweight, Rose Rhodochrosite on Malachite

With every move I have said goodbyes
to walls and keys and arms,
facing again familiar emptiness,
dizzied with the overripe-peach
aroma of fresh paint.

Moving out I clear the rooms, leaving
behind swirls with a quick vacuum,
sometimes dashing back to retrieve
a glove, a plane ticket, a comb.
My steps trace across the carpet
like imprints of a tango lesson,
question marks that will vanish
with the next vacuuming.

Every move has its own losses:
the small enamelled ring,
a photo of in-laws,
the jagged paperweight.

Were the in-laws tossed with the odd glove?
Did the ring fit another finger?
Has a strange hand turned over the card
and telephoned an unidentified number?
Has a finger stopped against the jagged
paperweight, sharp as a knife,
and held up to the light the rose
crystal slivered with green stones?

Postcard

Going back, I find
the slick surface.

The dead I write about
stand at the door calling.

They have a secret name for me.
On this side it sounds like
blocks of wood slamming together.

Life Messages: Horsewoman Dies

(*Washington Post*, May 18, 1989)

George Panagoulis, 78, Dies;
Was Prince George's Police Chief.

Church Founder (Was secretary to president).
Tutor, Teacher, Docent.
Development Banker.
Amateur Actress.
Private Duty Nurse.
Foreign Service Officer, at home.
Rockville First Grader.
Night Operator.
Horsewoman.

In Memoriam.
Cards of Thanks.

Notices:
Chapel, William R. (Bill)
On Monday
Charles, George J.
This is to notify
Brother George
Crawford, Winifred Mae (Winnie)
On Monday
David, Howard Nathan
(Hambone) On Friday
Dyson, Pleasant Virginia
Suddenly
Dyson, Virginia P.
Elk
McIntosh, C. Preston
with regret
Strong, Carolyn J.
Suddenly
White, "Baby Sis"
Saturday
Willis, James H.
Sunday
Zandonini, Elizabeth W.
Catholic Daughter
Zandonini, Elizabeth M.
On Tuesday

Lots
2 crypts/eighty-six hundred
Parklawn — 2 lots/Turf-topped
negotiable with vase/in granite
call home or office/call anytime
(lv. msge.)

A Fig Tree

for a nephew

I've planted a tree for you,
a cutting from a city where
neither of us has lived except
in old immigrants' afternoon dreams.

You never heard their broken voices.
You do not know what their sleep retrieves.
You find Spiderman easier to believe in
than my stories of their bravery, legends to you.
They wait at a safe distance, ghosts,
not touching you except through their names,
Old Country flowers, almost wilted, and
in our bodies, the New World fruits of theirs,
transplanted into the newest season.

You aren't yet awake to this dying,
the passing away of delicious fruit,
bees humming in our hair. You sit,
as I did, daydreaming, a child until
one of the old people surprises you by
running a piece of straw along your chin
and wakes you, laughing or crying.

If this tree lives and you like purple figs,
plant your own cutting wherever you want,
because I may be neither here nor there,
and anyway, nothing grows in one place forever.

Biographical Note

Leo Luke Marcello was born in DeRidder, Louisiana, in 1945. He has a B.A. from Tulane University and an M.A. and Ph.D. from Louisiana State University, with additional study at the University of Dallas and Catholic University of America. He is the author of *The Secret Proximity of Everywhere*, *Blackrobe's Love Letters*, and *Silent Film*. He edited and published *Everything Comes to Light: A Festschrift for Joy Scantlebury*. His awards include two Shearman Fellowships, a Shearman Endowed Professorship, a grant from the Louisiana Endowment for the Humanities, the Deep South Writers' Competition, and the David Lloyd Kreeger Award. He has taught at Howard University, Catholic University of America, and Louisiana State University and in Wales. He teaches in the Department of Languages of McNeese State University, in Lake Charles, Louisiana.

Also available from **Time Being Books**

EDWARD BOCCIA
No Matter How Good the Light Is: Poems by a Painter

LOUIS DANIEL BRODSKY
You Can't Go Back, Exactly
The Thorough Earth
Four and Twenty Blackbirds Soaring
Mississippi Vistas: Volume One of *A Mississippi Trilogy*
Falling from Heaven: Holocaust Poems of a Jew and a Gentile
    (with William Heyen)
Forever, for Now: Poems for a Later Love
Mistress Mississippi: Volume Three of *A Mississippi Trilogy*
A Gleam in the Eye: Poems for a First Baby
Gestapo Crows: Holocaust Poems
The Capital Café: Poems of Redneck, U.S.A.
Disappearing in Mississippi Latitudes: Volume Two of *A Mississippi Trilogy*
Paper-Whites for Lady Jane: Poems of a Midlife Love Affair
The Complete Poems of Louis Daniel Brodsky: Volume One, 1963–1967
Three Early Books of Poems by Louis Daniel Brodsky, 1967–1969: *The Easy Philosopher*, *"A Hard Coming of It" and Other Poems*, and *The Foul Rag-and-Bone Shop*
The Eleventh Lost Tribe: Poems of the Holocaust

HARRY JAMES CARGAS (editor)
Telling the Tale: A Tribute to Elie Wiesel on the Occasion of His 65th Birthday — Essays, Reflections, and Poems

JUDITH CHALMER
Out of History's Junk Jar: Poems of a Mixed Inheritance

GERALD EARLY
How the War in the Streets Is Won: Poems on the Quest of Love and Faith

ALBERT GOLDBARTH
A Lineage of Ragpickers, Songpluckers, Elegiasts & Jewelers: Selected Poems of Jewish Family Life, 1973–1995

ROBERT HAMBLIN
From the Ground Up: Poems of One Southerner's Passage to Adulthood

WILLIAM HEYEN
Erika: Poems of the Holocaust
Falling from Heaven: Holocaust Poems of a Jew and a Gentile
  (with Louis Daniel Brodsky)
Pterodactyl Rose: Poems of Ecology
Ribbons: The Gulf War — A Poem
The Host: Selected Poems, 1965–1990

TED HIRSCHFIELD
German Requiem: Poems of the War and the Atonement of a Third Reich Child

VIRGINIA V. JAMES HLAVSA
Waking October Leaves: Reanimations by a Small-Town Girl

RODGER KAMENETZ
The Missing Jew: New and Selected Poems
Stuck: Poems Midlife

NORBERT KRAPF
Somewhere in Southern Indiana: Poems of Midwestern Origins
Blue-Eyed Grass: Poems of Germany

ADRIAN C. LOUIS
Blood Thirsty Savages

GARDNER McFALL
The Pilot's Daughter

JOSEPH MEREDITH
Hunter's Moon: Poems from Boyhood to Manhood

BEN MILDER
The Good Book Says . . . : Light Verse to Illuminate the Old Testament

TIME BEING BOOKS
POETRY IN SIGHT AND SOUND

FOR OUR FREE CATALOG OR TO ORDER
(800) 331-6605 · FAX: (888) 301-9121 · http://www.timebeing.com